KID SCIENTIST
Astronauts on the Space Station

Sue Fliess
illustrated by Mia Powell

Albert Whitman & Company
Chicago, Illinois

For Owen and Wyatt, two brilliant stars in my galaxy—SF

Thank you to all of the astronauts who have traveled
beyond this world to discover the unknown—MP

Library of Congress Cataloging-in-Publication data
is on file with the publisher.

Text copyright © 2022 by Sue Fliess
Illustrations copyright © 2022 by Albert Whitman & Company
Illustrations by Mia Powell
First published in the United States of America
in 2022 by Albert Whitman & Company
ISBN 978-0-8075-4153-1 (hardcover)
ISBN 978-0-8075-4154-8 (ebook)

Printed in China
10 9 8 7 6 5 4 3 2 1 WKT 26 25 24 23 22

Design by Mary Freelove

For more information about Albert Whitman & Company,
visit our website at www.albertwhitman.com.

"We're locked on," says José, the crew's commander, as they dock the Soyuz spacecraft at the International Space Station, or ISS. The ISS is a human-made laboratory orbiting Earth at 17,000 miles per hour.

The astronauts' journey from Earth took two days, but José's small crew trained for two years for this mission: to live and conduct experiments in space. It's a dream come true!

"Great job!" says Jia.

"Open the hatch," says Cassie. The crew floats on board. Two Russian astronauts, called cosmonauts, who have been living in space greet the crew with an update about the ISS, wish them luck, and then depart back to Earth.

"We're in charge now," says José to his crew, "with the help of the scientists at NASA, of course." NASA is the US National Aeronautics and Space Administration.

The three move through the ISS modules, or rooms. They push off walls and handrails, swimming through the air. Jia somersaults. "Wheee!"

Back home, the force of gravity pulls everything toward the center of Earth, keeping humans from drifting away. In space, Earth's gravity keeps the ISS in orbit. But the space station itself is actually falling as it goes around the planet, making the astronauts feel weightless.

They head to the exercise module and check out the equipment. Each week, Cassie and Jia will observe how living in space affects the human body.

"I'll track our height, weight, and nutrition," says Jia.

"And I'll monitor our hearts," adds Cassie. Weightlessness can affect the heart's beating rhythm over time, so Cassie will be watching for any unusual patterns.

"Without gravity compressing our spines," says Jia, "our bodies might stretch out a bit too."

"So we may grow taller?" asks José.

Jia nods. "But our muscle size may decrease. In space, there's little resistance to help keep muscles in shape. We'll need to exercise regularly to stay healthy."

They look over their personalized workout plans.
"Two hours a day, six days a week?" asks José. "We'll be superheroes by the time we get home!"

Next, they review their food supply. Most space food is freeze-dried, which means all the water has been removed. The crew will add water to rehydrate the food before eating.

"I'll miss ice-cream sundaes," sighs Jia.

"Not so fast," says Cassie. "I found freeze-dried ice-cream sandwiches!"

PIZZA

CHICKEN NUGGETS

"Speaking of food," says José, "let's check out the Vegetable Production System module, or 'Veggie Lab.'"

José explains, "In my research I found that red lettuce has a good chance of growing in space because it doesn't need sunlight or soil to grow."

Instead of using direct sunlight, the Veggie Lab uses LED lights powered by solar panels, and José will use aeroponics, which is the process of growing plants without soil, in air or mist, while adding liquid nutrients.

RED LETTUCE

Cassie and Jia help José set up his plant-growing station.
"How long do you think it will take to grow?" asks Jia.
"My hypothesis, or guess based on evidence, is that it will take two months from seed to plant. Aeroponic plants often grow faster because they absorb more nutrients and the roots get more oxygen."

Over the next few weeks, the crew gets more comfortable living on the ISS. Cassie and Jia have logged hundreds of measurements, and José's lettuce has sprouted.

"I didn't think I'd be able to sleep standing up," says Jia. "But now I don't even miss my pillow."

Each astronaut has a sleeping bag that can be slept in on the floor, walls, or ceiling. In space, their bodies don't know which way is up or down!

"And I didn't think I'd get used to swallowing my toothpaste after brushing," says Cassie, "but we can't let water droplets float through the air and damage any equipment."

One morning, José announces,
"The lettuce has grown faster than
I expected!"

"So have I," says Jia. "I'm a
quarter of an inch taller!"

Suddenly, they hear an announcement:
"ISS, this is Mission Control. We've detected a large piece of space junk coming your way. It could either be a meteorite or hardware left from past space activity."

"Can we maneuver the ISS out of the way?" asks José.

"There's no time," says Mission Control. "Retreat to the spacecraft and wait it out."

"It sounds like this debris could cause real damage if it hits the station," says Cassie.

The crew quickly evacuates, hoping the debris misses them.

A few minutes later, Mission Control says, "We've detected an impact. There might be a damaged solar panel."

"Jia and I will check the panels and repair them if we can," says José.

"Without them, the plants might not survive," says Jia.

"The solar panels power the ISS," says Cassie. "We could lose more than plants if we can't make the repair."

REPAIR KIT

Cassie stays on board to help them navigate. José and Jia put on their spacesuits and helmets and attach tethers, which are long cables that prevent the astronauts from drifting into space.

"Ready?" asks Cassie.
The astronauts begin their spacewalk.

Quickly, José spots the problem.

"This panel is torn," he reports back.

The repair takes six hours, but they complete the job. Cassie updates NASA on the successful mission.

Before returning to the ISS, José and Jia stop to look at the stars.
"Space is awesome," says José.
Then they get safely back inside.

"Excellent work!" says José. "But there's still one thing to do."

"What's that?" asks Cassie.

"*Lettuce* celebrate!" says José, holding up three ice-cream sandwiches.

The crew continues to document everything about their journey, so when they return to Earth, they can present their findings and help NASA's future missions. They have learned so much...especially that while living in space, they have to be ready for anything.

WHAT IS AN ASTRONAUT?

The word *astronaut* comes from the Greek words *astron* and *nautes*, which mean "star" and "sailor." An astronaut is a scientist who goes through extensive training with the goal of traveling into outer space.

Astronauts have spacesuits that provide them with air and protect them from the extreme temperatures of space as well as from radiation from the sun. Most missions are led by a commander.

All scientists conduct research by following the steps of the scientific method. José and his crew used each step to guide their research.

STEPS OF THE SCIENTIFIC METHOD

1. Make an observation and do background research. Before José traveled to space, he researched what vegetation might have the best chance of growing in space.

2. Ask questions about the observations and gather information. José wondered how long it would take to grow the lettuce and, if it grew, whether it would be safe to eat.

3. Form a hypothesis. José hypothesized that it would take two months to grow lettuce in the Veggie Lab on the ISS.

4. Perform an experiment and collect data. José successfully grew lettuce in space, noted that it grew faster than he guessed it would, and planned to send it back to Earth to be tested for safe consumption.

5. Analyze the data and draw conclusions. Consider how the conclusions align with the hypothesis. José grew lettuce in space. If it is proven to be edible, his experiment would reveal that humans have a way to grow food off of Earth.

6. Communicate or present your findings. After gathering more data, José and his crew will publish what they learned about growing vegetables in space and how their bodies reacted to living in space so other scientists and astronauts can learn more about growing food and living on the International Space Station.

HOW CAN I BECOME AN ASTRONAUT?

Do you love space and learning about our solar system? Have you ever dreamed of living in space? Maybe you'll become an astronaut!

When you get older, if you decide you want to become an astronaut, you must have a college degree in engineering, life science, physical science, or mathematics. Being an astronaut has a lot of requirements. You need to be in great health, be good at math and science, have a good memory, be able to stay calm in difficult or scary situations, and be okay with heights and small spaces.

To become an astronaut, you have to apply to a space agency, like NASA. If you are chosen, you might train to work on the ISS, like José, Cassie, and Jia! Basic training can last six years. You learn how to fly spacecraft, repair all the equipment, and use basic medical skills. You could spend hundreds of hours practicing flight maneuvers in a simulator. You study many different fields, like navigation, meteorology, astronomy, physics, and more. Astronaut trainees also simulate space conditions by living without sunlight and practicing weightlessness in a swimming pool. After successfully completing training, candidates are designated NASA career astronauts!

Every year, thousands of people apply to NASA, but only a few become astronauts. You could be next!

There are many ways to learn about astronauts and living in space:

- Check out books or watch videos about space and the cosmos at your local library.
- Visit a planetarium or an air and space museum with your family. Sometimes there are interactive exhibits that let you experience what it would be like to go into space.
- Find out if you have an observatory near you. At an observatory, you can view the night sky—stars, moons, and planets—through dedicated visitor telescopes.

SUGGESTED READING FOR KIDS

Alkire, Jessie. *Scott Kelly: Remarkable Space Resident.* Minneapolis: Checkerboard Library, 2019.
Lawrence, Ellen. *Becoming an Astronaut.* New York: Bearport, 2019.
Nelson, Maria. *Life on the International Space Station.* New York: Gareth Stevens, 2013.